AF279216
MAY YOU ALWAYS KNOW

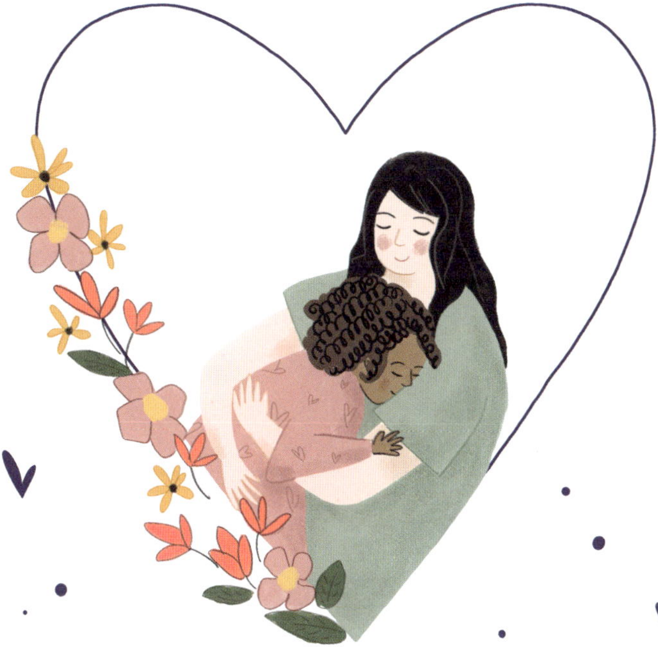

MAY YOU ALWAYS KNOW

A POEM OF HOPES AND DREAMS

Jessica Urlichs and Bethany Gale

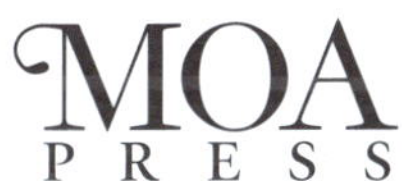

MOA PRESS

DEAREST LITTLE ONE,
I CAN'T WAIT TO WATCH YOU GROW.
AND THOUGH YOU'LL TEACH ME MORE,
HERE ARE SOME THINGS YOU OUGHT TO KNOW.

I'LL DO MY BEST TO GUIDE YOU,
I WILL HOLD YOUR HAND EACH DAY.
YOU WILL CREATE YOUR PATH
AND I'LL BE THE LAMPS ALONG THE WAY.

LOVE IS UNCONDITIONAL HERE,
YOU WILL ALWAYS BE SAFE WITH ME.
HOME CAN BE A PERSON TOO,
IN MY HEART YOU HOLD THE KEY.

YOU WON'T ALWAYS GET IT RIGHT
AND MISTAKES AREN'T ALWAYS WRONG.
LIFE IS FULL OF LEARNING,
GAINING WISDOM IS LIFELONG.

I PROMISE ON THE COLDEST DAYS
I'LL ALWAYS KEEP YOU WARM.
AS YOU DO THE SAME FOR ME
YOU ARE SUNSHINE IN HUMAN FORM.

LISTEN TO THAT VOICE INSIDE,
YOUR HEART IS GOOD, AND TRUE.
EVEN THOUGH THE WORLD IS ROUND,
IT CAN BE SHAPED BY YOU.

HOLD HEARTS AS WELL AS HANDS,
REACH OUT WITH ALL YOUR MIGHT,
THEN WRAP YOUR ARMS AROUND YOURSELF
REMEMBER TO HOLD ON TIGHT.

AT TIMES YOU MAY BE OVERWHELMED
AND IT WILL FEEL TOO MUCH.
DON'T FORGET TO TAKE A BREATH.
WHAT CAN YOU SEE? AND HEAR? AND TOUCH?

YOU'RE ACHIEVING MORE THAN YOU THINK
WHETHER YOU WALK OR RUN.
I HOPE WHEN YOU LOOK BACK,
YOU SEE JUST HOW FAR YOU'VE COME.

YOU'LL NEVER GO WRONG WITH FLOWERS,
BETTER YET, IS LENDING AN EAR.
A FEELING CAN LAST A LIFETIME,
REMEMBER THOSE WHO WERE THERE.

I'VE ALWAYS KNOWN YOU CAN DO IT,
DON'T TELL YOURSELF YOU CAN'T.
BECAUSE THOUGHTS WILL GROW IF YOU FEED THEM,
SO BE CAREFUL WHAT YOU PLANT.

SOME DAYS YOU'LL WALK ON SUNSHINE,
OTHERS YOU'LL FEEL THE STRAIN.
THERE WILL ALWAYS BE A RAINBOW,
PLEASE LOOK FOR IT IN THE RAIN.

REMEMBER TO LISTEN TO OTHERS,
YOU CAN CHANGE A LIFE BEING KIND.
YOU CAN KEEP YOUR POINT OF VIEW
AND STILL KEEP AN OPEN MIND.

DON'T COMPARE YOURSELF TO OTHERS,
YOU ARE PERFECT AS YOU ARE.
NOURISH AND LOVE YOUR BODY
SO IT CAN TAKE YOU FAR.

YOU CAN'T CHANGE OTHER PEOPLE,
BE REAL WHEN THINGS SEEM FAKE.
FOR ONLY YOU CAN CHANGE YOURSELF
AND THE ACTIONS THAT YOU TAKE.

YOU WON'T BE GREAT AT EVERYTHING
AND THERE IS NO NEED TO BE.
BUT YOU WILL BE GREAT AT MANY THINGS,
YOUR PASSIONS WILL SET YOU FREE.

HAPPINESS IS NOT A DESTINATION,
OR A RACE TO A FINISH LINE.
IT'S A COLLECTION OF BEAUTIFUL MOMENTS
AND THEY HAPPEN ALL THE TIME.

STAND UP FOR WHAT YOU BELIEVE IN,
SHINE BRIGHT AND SPREAD THAT GLOW.
BRAVE IS SAYING YES
AND BRAVE IS ALSO SAYING NO.

CLIMATE CHANGE
STOP
SAVE OUR PLANET
THERE IS NO PLANET B
HEAR OUR VOICE

REMEMBER TO LOVE WITHOUT BORDERS,
YOU DON'T NEED TO HAVE A THICK SKIN.
IF YOU BUILD ARMOUR AROUND YOUR HEART,
YOU WILL NEVER LET TRUE LOVE IN.

KEEP ON ASKING QUESTIONS,
BE CURIOUS, BE OUTSPOKEN.
YOUR HEART WILL TELL YOU RIGHT FROM WRONG,
SOME RULES ARE MEANT TO BE BROKEN.

FIND PEOPLE YOU CAN DEPEND ON,
SHOULDERS ON WHICH TO LEAN.
THOSE WHO LOVE YOU FOR WHO YOU ARE
SHOW YOU WHAT TRUE FRIENDSHIP MEANS.

EVERYBODY CRIES SOMETIMES,
FOR TEARS ARE SENT TO HEAL.
LET THEM ROLL DOWN YOUR CHEEKS,
YOUR HEART WAS MADE TO FEEL.

I'LL ALWAYS BE YOUR SAFE PLACE,
LONG AFTER YOU ARE SMALL.
EVEN IF YOU CAN'T SEE ME,
I WILL COME TO YOU WHEN YOU CALL.

IT'S OKAY FOR THINGS TO CHANGE,
WE ARE MEANT TO GROW THROUGH SEASONS.
WHAT'S MEANT FOR YOU WILL STAY, MY LOVE,
ALWAYS TRUST THERE IS A REASON.

THOSE TWINKLING STARS ARE NOT THAT FAR,
AIM HIGH AND CHASE YOUR DREAMS.
YOUR FEARS WILL RISE LIKE A RIVERBANK
SO DARLING, BE THE STREAM.

THERE IS SO MUCH TO LOOK FORWARD TO,
I CAN'T WAIT TO WATCH YOU GROW.
YOU'RE BRAVE, YOU'RE LOVED, YOU'RE WONDERFUL.
MAY YOU ALWAYS KNOW.

To my children, and whoever is reading this: may you always know.

To my little rays of sunshine. Being your auntie is one of the greatest gifts. May you always know how much I love you.

Jessica is a New Zealand poet who has three children and loves writing about the ordinary being extraordinary. You can find Jessica on Instagram @jessurlichs.

Bethany Gale is an Urban Designer and Illustrator with a passion for bringing ideas to life through her drawings. Originally from the UK, Bethany is now based in Te Whanganui a Tara Wellington. You can find Bethany on Instagram @bybethanygale.

MOA
PRESS

Published in New Zealand and Australia in 2025 by Moa Press
(an imprint of Hachette Aotearoa New Zealand Limited)
Level 2, 23 O'Connell Street, Auckland, New Zealand
www.moapress.co.nz
www.hachette.co.nz

A catalogue record for this book is available from the National Library of New Zealand.

978-1-86971-564-9 (hardback)

Cover and internal design by Kinart Ltd
Printed in China by 1010 Printing International Ltd